D1626756

CANCEL

The British at Home

The Way We Were

The British at Home

TIM GLYNNE-JONES

ARCTURUS

ARCTURUS

This edition published in 2016 by Arcturus
Publishing Limited
26/27 Bickels Yard, 151–153 Bermondsey Street,
London SE1 3HA

Copyright © Arcturus Holdings Limited

All rights reserved. No part of this publication
may be reproduced, stored in a retrieval system,
or transmitted, in any form or by any means,
electronic, mechanical, photocopying, recording
or otherwise, without prior written permission in
accordance with the provisions of the Copyright
Act 1956 (as amended). Any person or persons
who do any unauthorised act in relation to this
publication may be liable to criminal prosecution
and civil claims for damages.

ISBN: 978-1-78428-296-7
AD005269UK

Cover design: Maki Ryan

Printed in China

Contents

Introduction

We all have a clear image of 'the Brits abroad', but what about the British at home? How has the British way of life been shaped over the last century and what have been the significant influences? This book turns the lens on an extraordinary era in British history, from the 1920s to the 1970s – a time that saw fundamental changes in our expectations of life and established certain social patterns that are familiar to us today but would have been entirely alien to our Victorian predecessors.

It was a time of rapid modernization, the era when cars, washing machines, vacuum cleaners and televisions came from non-existence to being part of everyday life. Attitudes changed from Victorian-style morality to rock'n'roll irreverence; the stiff upper lip started to quiver a little; obedient children became juvenile delinquents; and the respect for one's elders fell into the 'generation gap'. These were the growing pains of a Britain in search of freedom, for the right to self-expression and equal opportunities. It was a time that saw widespread improvements in our standard of living – but at a price!

In the middle of it all came the most destructive war in the history of the planet. The Second World War put the brakes on Britain's social development but, like a coiled spring, it burst forth again in peace time. A look back at those days throws up charming recollections of a time gone by but also throws light on the seismic changes that formed the domestic landscape of today.

Queen Mary's dolls house gives a behind-closed-doors glimpse into how the other half lived in the 1920s. The wonderfully detailed model features all the trappings of the upper class British household: a large library on the ground floor, a huge, high-ceilinged master bedroom on the first floor, with servants' quarters tucked away at the top and sides, from where they could attend to the master and mistress of the house in no time flat. Most impressive is the 'garage' of limousines in the basement, complete with motorbike and sidecar and a rather fine-looking lawnmower.

Days of Hope

But the average British household was a far cry from such grandeur. Only the wealthy could afford a car, let alone five; indeed, most people deemed themselves lucky if they had hot and cold running water. But times were changing. The 1930s would see the rapid expansion of suburbia and the rehousing of inner-city families to new dwellings with modern conveniences. The electrification of Britain's households was under way, bringing light and power to domestic life, paving the way for new inventions such as television, vacuum cleaners and washing machines. For most households, such luxuries would have to wait until after the Second World War, but the shape of things to come was more than just a child's imagination.

Two young lads, just home from school, eat their tea of a 'doorstep' of bread and jam on the front doorstep of their house. Bread was the main staple for most British households and a good, thick 'doorstep' would keep the wolf from the door until supper time.

If you had to get up particularly early for work in 1929, you didn't set an alarm clock, you paid a 'knocker-up' like Charles Nelson from Hoxton here, to come round and tap on your bedroom window with a long stick. The question is, who woke Charles?

A young follower of Charlie Chaplin keeps the crowd amused in his local community in east London. Chaplin was a household name and a hero of the British working classes, some of whom dreamed of making the same rags to riches escape from poverty as he had.

Left *Mrs Thomson, a resident of Kinver Edge in Worcestershire, where troglodytes lived in houses carved out of the red sandstone until the 1960s. One of the last rock-dwellers in British history, Mrs Thomson had lived in this home for 50 years when the photograph was taken in 1935.*

Above *With one or two small changes, such as the style of the streetlamps and the design of the car, this is a timeless scene from British suburbia: a couple washing their car outside the family semi. Taken some time around 1930, it shows the style of architecture that boomed between the wars.*

A huntsman outside Mentmore House in Buckinghamshire partakes of some liquid refreshment while the hounds wait patiently to be unleashed on the trail of a fox. The hunt was a staunch British tradition among the upper classes and agricultural communities, who regarded foxes as nothing but a threat to their livestock.

The receding shores of Britain's South Coast have forced the closure of the old tea house on the edge of Black Rock, Brighton as a new promenade is built below it. The house is in imminent danger of collapse as the cliff face is eroded by the sea and has been earmarked for demolition.

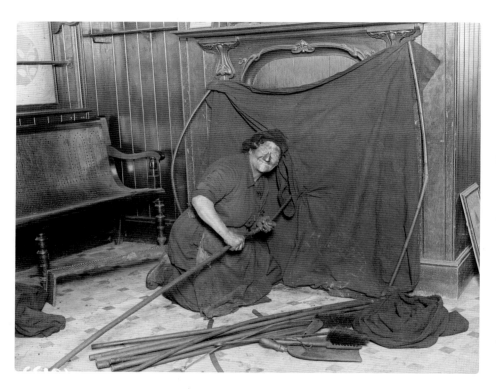

A female chimney sweep goes about her business in Clapton, east London, feeding the brush up the flue through a carefully arranged protective cloth. In 1928, sweeps were in constant demand, with most homes relying on solid fuel fires to keep them warm and provide heat for cooking.

Sitting by this fireplace is a picture of refined elegance, a debutante all dressed up for her presentation at Buckingham Palace. The ostrich feather head dress and white dress with long, flowing train were standard attire, symbolizing the virginity of the 17-year-old debs as they took their place in 'society' for the first time.

Left *A pair of decorators touch up the paintwork around the doorway of Stanley Baldwin's house. Baldwin lived at No.10 Downing Street in three spells as Prime Minister between 1923 and 1937, during which time he was obliged to make sure the traditional London residence was kept ship shape.*

Right *A mother and her daughters pose for the camera as men from their street put up a banner proclaiming a 'Children's Coronation Party' to celebrate the coronation of King George VI in 1937. Any excuse to get the patriotic bunting out was enthusiastically taken up in Britain's close-knit urban communities.*

A nation of pet lovers

A reptile fancier exhibits her collection of chameleons, just one of the many weird and wonderful species that could be found in British homes. Britain had long been known as a 'nation of animal lovers' due to an affinity with our furry and feathered friends that dated back to the Victorian era. Britain had been the first country to establish an animal welfare charity (the RSPCA) and the Kennel Club had been founded in 1873, primarily to regulate the dog shows that were growing in popularity.

Dogs, cats, birds and fish were common fare, but the hobbyist tendencies of the British led them to keep more adventurous creatures. Lizards, snakes, spiders and even the more aggressive carnivores were all available to buy and the British snapped them up. The simple home became an aviary, an aquarium, a vivarium and more, with tanks and cages housing the exotic beasts that evolution had spared from existence in the hostile British climate.

Above *At home a simple costermonger, in public a Pearly King with his Pearly Queen and Pearly Prince and Princess. The Cockney custom of Pearly Kings and Queens kept many a London family busy, sewing mother of pearl buttons on to their dress clothes, to be worn on special occasions.*

Right *A group of young women dressed as fish enjoy an invigorating cup of tea in a very well appointed sitting room, in preparation for the Chelsea Arts Ball, one of the more lavish occasions in the social calendar. Girls getting together to prepare for parties was de rigueur.*

Men from the Derbyshire town of Ashbourne get stuck in during the annual game of Shrovetide football, a Medieval tradition that pitted men from opposite ends of the town against each other on Shrove Tuesday, in a supposedly sporting contest that would turn violent at the drop of a hat.

A maid prepares tea in the kitchen of the R100 airship, which will be her home for the duration of the 78-hour flight to Canada, made in the summer of 1930. The flight was successful, but soon afterwards her sister ship, the R101, crashed in France and the airship was decommissioned.

At a time when fewer than one in five British households had electric power, a porter at London's Savoy Hotel proudly demonstrates a new electric lift that has been installed to improve the efficiency of the cloakroom facilities. Hats, coats and umbrellas are whisked away at the push of a button.

Picnickers at the Epsom Derby gather round a spread that appears to consist of Champagne, pies, sausages and a large cucumber. Derby Day was one of the first big events in the English 'summer season' and would bring out the posh picnic hampers and aproned serving staff regardless of the weather.

Two thatchers ply their craft on the roof of a traditional country cottage. Thatching was a dying art between the wars as thatched roofs became associated with rural poverty and homeowners chose alternative methods for keeping the weather out. The beauty and eco-friendliness of thatch were largely unappreciated.

The two ends of the social scale rub shoulders as Durham miners welcome HRH The Prince of Wales to their humble homes during a Royal tour of the North-East. The popular prince would later become King Edward VIII, albeit briefly, before abdicating in 1936.

Above *What a shot! A budding young cricketer follows the flight of his majestic on drive as his chums in the slips remain crouched in anticipation and the local girls look on in admiration. The street was your playground and your imagination provided the arena, before the call went up to come in for tea.*

Right *A smartly dressed resident of Morden in south London returns home from work on his bicycle, with his dog perched parrot-like on his shoulder. For most British workers, cycling was the luxury method of travelling to and from work, the alternative being Shanks's Pony (aka walking).*

All mod cons

The 1932 North London Exhibition at Alexandra Palace unveils a design classic – the typical 1930s suburban house. This was the architectural model that would house Britain's growing middle classes for decades to come, a spacious, well-appointed dwelling fit for modern living.

The proliferation of these houses, particularly around London and the South-East, was due to a monetary policy of low interest rates aimed at kick-starting an economic recovery following the Great Depression. The policy worked and the number of owner-occupied houses in Britain increased by around 2.5 million.

Residents from inner London were encouraged out to the suburbs, where they found far more spacious homes than they were used to selling for under £500 and theirs for a down payment of just £1. The exodus was under way. Home ownership was the sign of the country's growing prosperity and the more insular suburban estate was replacing the communal character of the terraced street.

Tiaras and ball gowns are the order of the day as friends and neighbours gather for an occasion in the 1930s, possibly a New Year's Eve party. The scarcity of men among the crowd was indicative of the imbalance between the sexes brought about by the carnage of the First World War.

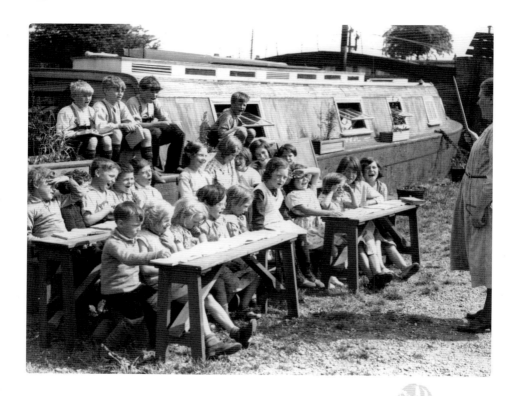

'The sun is shining so we can have lessons outdoors today!' These children actually lived on board barges on the Grand Union Canal at West Drayton, Middlesex, and took their education at a special barge school, where al fresco lessons were quite commonplace.

Unemployed miners with a collecting tin labelled 'Please help' stop for a drink from their tin cups and a bite of bread during a hunger march in 1930. The Great Depression ravaged the coal industry and left whole communities without work and forced to march to London to raise awareness of their plight.

Left *Smartly dressed players cover their faces with masks at a suburban card party. The masks are intended to conceal any facial expressions giving away what is in their hand.*

Right *A woman demonstrates a newfangled hair steaming machine at the annual Hair Dressing Exhibition at White City. For the well-to-do woman at home, it made light work of applying the elegant wavy-haired look made popular by the likes of actress Jean Harlow.*

On the Rise

With the dark days of the First World War more than a decade behind them and the country climbing out from the depths of the Great Depression, the British home became a place of modern comfort and joy for increasing numbers of people. Where once it had been a constant daily effort to heat and light the family home, now darkness and cold could be banished at the flick of a switch.

Moreover, such convenience was no longer the preserve of the rich. Domestic comfort was becoming the norm for many people, and that first taste of luxury led to a demand for more. Industry duly obliged with a stream of modern appliances and toys to satisfy the growing hunger for the good life.

In this picture, a couple from London take a dip in a swimming pool on the roof of their Oxford Street flat.

An extremely middle-class family in Richmond, Surrey takes tea in the garden. The 1930s was the age of Britain's middle classes, in which the economy strengthened and prosperity came within reach of a large swathe of the population, who began to enjoy, and expect, a higher standard of living.

Patients and nurses at Moorfields Eye Hospital in London listen to the football on the radio with the visual aid of a blackboard. The pitch divided into squares was used as a reference by radio commentators to indicate to listeners where the ball was at any given time. It gave rise to the phrase 'Back to square one'.

She's all-electric

A model at Harrods in 1933 has the enviable job of demonstrating a range of new electrical gadgets for the home. A table lamp, a clock, a wireless and a kettle are all part of the display, bringing the ultimate in convenience right to your bedside.

Although electric street lighting had been in operation since the late 19th century, the electrification of British homes was a slow process. By the 1930s the National Grid was in operation but only one household in five had electricity. Nevertheless, that was enough to set the domestic appliance industry in motion. For the well-off patrons of Harrod's, such conveniences were the natural next step in the modernization of their well-appointed homes and demand for new gadgets was high.

By the outbreak of the Second World War, three-quarters of British households owned an electric iron and more and more people were following the news on their electric radio or, for the privileged few, television.

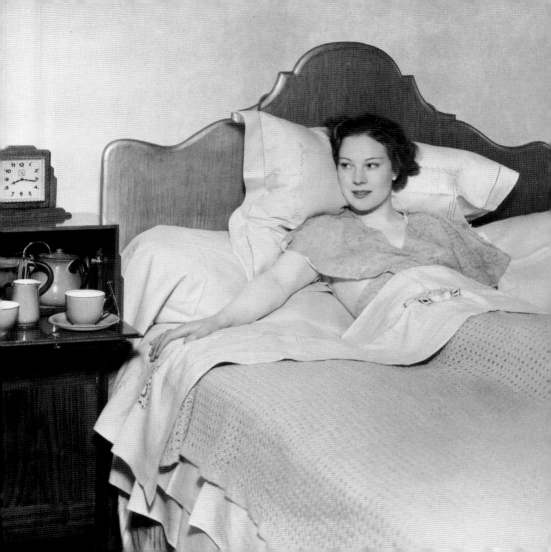

The crowds turn out in large numbers in 1938 for the visit of Queen Mary, wife of George V, to Brixton to open an extension to Lambeth Town Hall. The photographer has zeroed in on some of the few black faces in the crowd at the time. They were forerunners of the West Indian and African immigrants who were to arrive in Brixton in the 1940s and 1950s.

Cricket fans outside Lord's look on as a young Etonian escorts
his sisters to the ground for the Annual Cricket Festival between
Eton and Harrow, the country's two foremost public schools.
The annual cricket match was up there with the Boat Race as a
major fixture in the sporting calendar in the 1930s.

A cold snap opens up another opportunity for people to come outdoors as a frozen pond becomes an impromptu ice rink for the residents of Hampstead, London. It was cold back then. In rural parts of the country farmers would flood their fields in winter to create huge ice rinks for the locals to come and enjoy.

Guests at a dinner thrown by the Standard Motor Company in Coventry in 1936 react with typical British reserve as a line of motor cars parades through their banquet – not something you see every day. Nevertheless, a number of diners behave as if nothing unusual is taking place.

'Lor' love a duck! What's all this then?' A milkman scratches his head
in bemusement at the sight of shop dummies being carried into the
Victoria & Albert Museum in London. Exposure to the more outré
aspects of life and art was limited for most of the population.

Keeping up with the Joneses! Neighbours can't help showing their admiration as Bert Williams, head gardener at Berrington Hall in Ludlow, applies his skills to the 300-year-old piece of topiary known as 'The Peahen and Her Eggs'. Around the country, countless surburban gardeners carried on their own rivalries with similar creations.

Above *A dual carriageway in Ilford, north London, built in the 1930s. The street is lined with the classic suburban 1930s houses, with mock Tudor gable ends, bay windows and front gardens divided by hedges. With admirable foresight, the wide road has been constructed in readiness for the impending deluge of private cars.*

Right *Meanwhile, the 'old money' with exotic names continued to live in the peaceful surrounds of their country piles. This is Lynden Manor in Berkshire, home to Nadejda Mountbatten (centre), Marchioness of Milford Haven, with her daughter Tatiana and son David enjoying a game of croquet.*

Before sport became a religion, it was enthusiastically embraced by the clergy. At a time when future popes were playing football, Reverend Pat McCormack, the Vicar of St Martin in the Fields, London draws a big crowd for a celebration cricket match in the churchyard.

High spirits abound at a street party in St John's Wood, London, to celebrate the Coronation of King George VI in 1937. The Punch and Judy Show was a favourite entertainment for children, usually reserved for trips to the seaside, but brought into town for the big occasion.

Long before the days of Trick or Treat, children were placated on Halloween with a toffee apple. An orb of healthy goodness coated in a crispy sweet glaze, the toffee apple served the dual purpose of making children happy and gluing their jaws together so they couldn't complain even if they wanted to.

Eccentricity was alive and well in Britain between the wars. This amateur astronomer, accompanied by his young protégée, decides that the middle of the road is the best place from which to photograph the total eclipse of the sun that took place in June 1936. Well, there wasn't much traffic about…

Being British meant taking part in strange events in public places, usually in costume. These schoolgirls are dressed as Egyptians for the 1936 Pageant of Empire, an annual festival in which thousands of people celebrated the British Empire by re-enacting moments from history.

Is the grass greener on the other side? Passers-by, both young and old,
are drawn by the irresistible allure of peering through a crack in a fence to
appease their curiosity as to what's happening on the other side. In this case
it just happens to be the 1938 Wimbledon Tennis Championships.

Residents of Hungerford enact the local Hock Day tradition of demanding a kiss from the local women. Hock Day, or Hocktide, was a Medieval custom that involved the women reciprocating by tying up the men and demanding money for their release, which they then donated to the local church.

If domestic life was becoming increasingly comfortable and convenient, when you ventured out it remained a battle for survival! At least, you had to wrap up against the elements, like this heroic motoring party embarking on a drive to Monte Carlo for the famous rally.

Keep Calm and Carry On

By the mid-1930s, when this picture was taken, Britain was enjoying a wave of prosperity the likes of which had never been seen before, but, like those early racing cars, just as it all seemed to be going so well, a nasty clanging noise and a cloud of black smoke signalled the end of all the fun – Hitler was on the rise.

By the time war broke out in 1939, Britain was resigned to the conflict and ready to dig in. Aircraft meant the threat to house and home would come from the skies, and so home moved underground. In spite of the constant threat, the bulldog spirit grew stronger as those left at home fought their own war to preserve the British way of life at all costs.

Takeaway dinners

Customers queue to buy 'hot fish and chips' from a mobile vendor in Caledonian Market, London. The race was then on to get them home before they became 'cold fish and chips'. The concept of takeaway food didn't exist before the Second World War, but feeding the family from the fish and chip van or shop was commonplace, especially on Fridays.

The national dish hit its peak of popularity in the 1930s, with around 30,000 fish and chip shops in operation throughout the country. During the war, fish and chips was one dish that escaped rationing, although fish could be hard to come by. If the word went out that the local chippy had fish, long queues would form and Mum would rub her hands in glee at the thought of not having to cook that night.

A 1937 garden fete in Peckham, London, provides a chance for fathers to let their hair down – what little they have of it – and show their fun side in the donkey derby. Still stiffly dressed in jackets and ties, they seem to be giving plenty of amusement to those looking on.

Pride in your neighbourhood ran deep. No matter how poor you were, you could still dress your street up for the big occasion. Street parties like this brought communities together and cemented the bond that existed among those close-knit houses.

'I'll be mother.' Tea time in a typical British home was traditionally taken early in the evening before the house fell dark and would bring every member of the household to the table to eat, drink and share their accounts of the day.

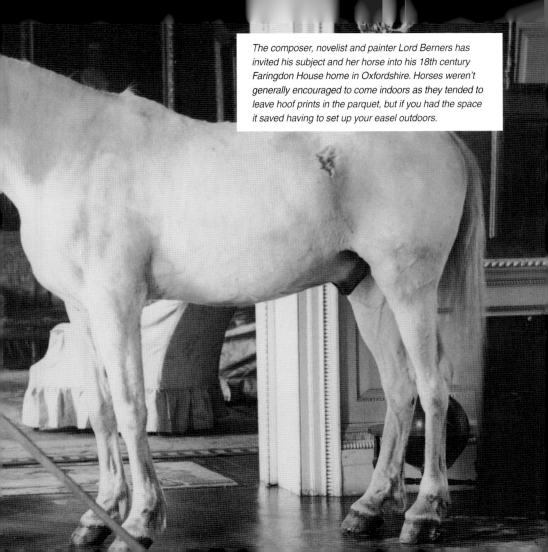

The composer, novelist and painter Lord Berners has invited his subject and her horse into his 18th century Faringdon House home in Oxfordshire. Horses weren't generally encouraged to come indoors as they tended to leave hoof prints in the parquet, but if you had the space it saved having to set up your easel outdoors.

The general trend was towards bigger, more comfortable houses, but there were always exceptions. This man is the proud owner of the smallest house in Scotland in 1939 – effectively a shed, from which he has hung large rocks to prevent it being blown away by gales.

Deportment was important in social circles and well-heeled girls learnt how to stand up straight at finishing schools like this one, the Lucie Clayton College in London. Also a modelling agency, Lucie Clayton prepared girls in posture, etiquette and charm, so they could carry themselves with grace and become 'good catches'.

Football was the working man's release, a place to club together and let off steam after the week (and in many cases the Saturday morning) at work. Most supporters lived within easy reach of the club they followed and the terraces became an extension of the local community.

These two babies appear to be acutely aware of the gathering storm in Europe in 1939 – or maybe they're just cross about being caged in. For them home life has been disrupted by evacuation to the countryside at the start of the Second World War and they're not happy about it.

This millworker from Ashton-under-Lyne makes the point that it's not just the wealthy who can keep large quadrupeds about the house. His donkey, Billy, is given the run of the place but, like most donkeys, he never knows where to draw the line.

Left *Tea brings this family to the table of their new council flat in Hackney, London, built for the slum clearance effort that stemmed from the 1930 Housing Act. The new flats meant a marked improvement in living conditions for many Londoners and the landing replaced the street as the place to meet.*

Right *At the other end of the social scale, tea is taken out of the home and into the car – in this case a Wolseley, fitted with fold-out trays. Having realized that the motor car could open the door to whole new horizons, manufacturers embarked on the process of making them as comfortable as home.*

Women queue up to shoot Nazis during the Second World War – or at least, to get some target practice just in case the enemy should ever land on British soil. The strength of the domestic matriarch would now be called upon in ensuring the defence of the realm.

Left *With a modicum of creativity, you could create beauty and elegance in the humblest of locations. This green-fingered 80-year-old from Camberwell, south-east London, has turned an old gramophone speaker into a plant-holder, adding a touch of panache to his window box garden.*

Above *Was it tea that won the war? The determination to drink a cuppa whatever the circumstances certainly seemed to symbolize the bulldog spirit. In this picture, a pool full of bathers from Droitwich take a break from swimming to partake of a refreshing brew.*

Have wheels, will travel. An example of the newly mobilized middle classes, this man looks particularly eager to hit the road, while his wife and six children look somewhat more circumspect. Still, it's better than walking and if it makes it to the seaside, all will have been worthwhile.

A butler goes about his business on the covered terrace of a stately home, preparing to serve refreshments. The role of the British butler, as typified by PG Wodehouse's Jeeves, was to maintain a lofty air of unshakeable competence and subtle condescension.

Crowds taking shelter from German bombs at Aldwych Underground station in 1940 spill on to the tracks in search of somewhere to make themselves comfortable. The Underground became a home from home for many Londoners during the Blitz, and served as a place for the never-say-die wartime spirit to grow strong.

An Air Raid Warden brandishes a wooden rattle to warn of a possible gas attack. Everyone around has dutifully fitted their gas masks, which they were obliged to carry everywhere during the Blitz. The wooden rattle had been used to warn of gas during the First World War and became a popular accessory on the football terraces.

A volunteer from Lever Brothers hands out towels to a queue of youngsters waiting for their turn in the tub. When domestic washing facilities were destroyed or rendered unusable, the mobile bath unit moved in to make sure the children of London washed behind their ears.

'I can't hear you!' War is miles from the minds of these children as they join in as one with the Christmas entertainment being provided by this clown and his cohorts in 1941. Many firms laid on shows for the children of employees and the spirit in the room was enough to conquer Hitler on its own.

Hammocks strung between railway lines provide a cosy bed for three children in their new makeshift London home. The frequency of the air raids during the Blitz drove some families to take up residence in the Tube at nights and it was a long time before many children would wake up in their own bed again.

In a scene typical of wartime, a sailor reaches over a picket fence to kiss 'the girl next door'. Countless relationships ended in this way, but this picture was taken in 1945 when the boys were coming home, ready to rekindle those romances that absence had made all the more intense.

From the 1950s onwards, Britain set about shaking off the grim shroud of the Second World War. It was a more forward-thinking country, one in which technology was making life less labour-intensive by the day, and as people found themselves with more leisure time,

Living the Dream

they began to dream way beyond their familiar domestic horizons.

The era began with a new Queen, a symbol of youth and beauty for an age of innovation and style. People moved in their millions from rundown terraced streets to new suburban council houses and futuristic tower blocks. They found themselves with gardens to tend, allotments in which to grow food, cars with which to get around and televisions to keep them indoors.

For the first time in their lives, many people found they had choice – especially women, who had shown during the war that they had much more to offer society than their domestic skills and now wanted the freedom to explore their options outside the home. Some men embraced the change, others took fright and ran to the pub, where they found cigarette machines and juke boxes playing rock'n'roll.

With the war out of the way, the playing fields of Eton could return to the business of producing accomplished sportsmen. In bright summer sunshine, 1947, a group of pupils take some tips from their tennis coach on serving technique.

'First we'll have a cup of tea.' A group from the Women's Institute take a well-deserved break during a canning session in the village hall at Ashton-under-Edge. While the WI continued to specialize in traditionally 'womanly' pursuits, it became a bastion of the female power that was gathering strength postwar.

Above *Whose idea do you think this was? While most people are making plans to buy their own motor car, Mr Dado treats his wife to a drive down the road in his cycle-powered car. The British appetite for invention and eccentricity came through the war in good shape.*

Right *'Can you lift your feet up, pet?' A woman treats her home to a once-over with one of those newfangled electric vacuum cleaners, while her wire-haired terrier does his best to avoid being sucked up. People liked to use brand names for these new devices, and so the vacuum cleaner became the 'hoover'.*

Somewhere in Yorkshire, 1950, local men line up outside the pub waiting for opening time. The pub was a male bastion, a place to get away from the wife, but the licensing laws restricted opening times to a few hours around lunch and then a few hours in the evening.

Above *As dog shows and dog breeding grew in popularity, it became apparent that people were starting to look like their dogs – a phenomenon that is exemplified in this picture of owners from the Pekingese Club with their bow-legged pets at the club's annual championship in London.*

Right *In an English country garden in 1952, Hollywood actress Lynn Fontanne tends the magnolias, while her husband and co-star Alfred Lunt checks for clouds before settling down to a quiet afternoon's reading in the sun. The cinema industry created a new aristocracy with the money to live like royalty.*

Up on a hill above the local colliery, a team of men dig an allotment. The limited self-sufficiency afforded by an allotment had had a staunch following before the war but the Dig For Victory campaign exposed more people to the joys of growing your own and the demand for allotments increased in the postwar years.

Customers at one of London's many jellied eel stalls in 1951. The Cockney staple was about to be joined by a whole new selection of eating out options, including American-style burger bars like Wimpy, which first opened in 1954, and all manner of ethnic cuisines courtesy of the postwar wave of immigrants from around the Commonwealth.

The average domestic household consisted of 2.4 children but this family bucked the trend somewhat. The prolific Charles and Elizabeth Hudson lie buried somewhere beneath their 20 children and six grandchildren, all transfixed by the television in their eight-room Victorian house in London, 1953.

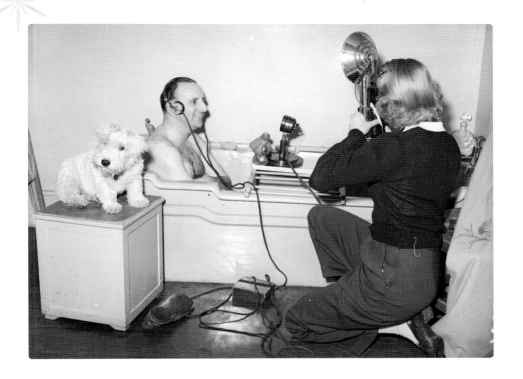

Always one for a spot of hijinx, the legendary cricket commentator and television broadcaster Brian Johnston takes the concept of working from home to a new dimension. While taking electronic equipment into the bath wasn't advisable, the picture represents the expanding reach of broadcast media in all corners of daily life.

In 1953 the country came outdoors for another Coronation. This time it was the turn of Queen Elizabeth II, a female monarch for a female age. By comparison with the celebrations of 1937, Britain was in a somewhat more raucous party mood, as epitomised by these two revellers, clinging on to their vantage point along the processional route.

The last vestiges of Victorian reserve had been swept away by the war.
This was a Britain where the ingrained sense of humour and the absurd
was being given free rein again, coupled with a sense of national pride
that meant any Royal occasion became a cue for a party.

Post-war kids, dressed in tiaras and red, white and blue hats, get their first taste of the traditional street party in London's East End – they were celebrating the Coronation in 1953 – while the grown-ups line the pavement and a seated man takes it all in from his front doorstep.

Oi, there's a queue

The very British art of queuing is expertly demonstrated by commuters at a bus stop in Leatherhead, Surrey. Man at front reads newspaper; man behind tries to read it over his shoulder; the rest gaze in different directions to avoid having to talk to one another.

While the discipline of queuing is believed to date back to the early 19th century, when the poor were made to stand in line for hand-outs, the Second World War brought a dignity to the custom, as it came to symbolize the selflessness, fair play and sense of hope that was necessary to keep order during wartime. During the years of rationing, people often joined a queue without knowing what it was leading to!

After the war the custom continued as an act of common decency, for which the British were both admired and mocked, even from within.

Left *A lighthouse keeper and his wife welcome a rare visitor to their remote home on the Highland coast. There were hundreds of manned lighthouses in the 1950s, some in which the keepers would work in shifts, other, more accessible ones, where the keepers set up home for life.*

Right *Two lads from Harrogate pose proudly looking up to an even higher camera from the branches of their treehouse. Trees were made for climbing and a nation of boys inspired by the adventures of Tarzan took to the lofty heights to build their own jungle playgrounds.*

Fred Astaire? Bing Crosby? No, it's Joe Lucy Jnr, son of the British lightweight boxing champion Joe Lucy, cutting a dash among his East End chums as he prepares to show his face at a wedding. The influence of Hollywood was strong among the younger generation.

British marbles champion Bert Paradine of the Arundel Mullets takes on a member of the Tinsley Green Tigers at the World Marbles Championship. Marbles at Tinsley Green, Sussex, had become a longstanding tradition, with roots stretching back to 1588. In 1951, the British Marbles Board of Control was formed with its HQ at the village's Greyhound pub.

The ladies are not for turning! This formidable-looking crowd have donned their hats to gather for the 28th Conservative Women's National Advisory Committee Conference at Central Hall, Westminster in 1956. Key issues of the day included prostitution, homosexuality and those dreadful rock and roll teenagers.

Above *The amount of time people spent at home was decreasing while the amount of time they spent in their cars was on the rise. And increasingly they found they weren't actually going anywhere. The traffic jam had become a regular blot on the British way of life.*

Right *Dad sits in the comfy chair, Mum smokes a cigarette and everyone stares expressionless at the goggle box. Where the dinner table had been the place for the family to convene, now it was the living room, in front of the television – except nobody looked at one another and barely a word was exchanged.*

Left *'Your mother warned you what would happen if you went down there!' A boy takes his game of Cowboys and Indians, inspired by Saturday morning cinema, to a sooty extreme as he takes cover in the coal chute of his house. Fortunately, his friend wasn't riding his bike along the pavement at the time!*

Right *By 1957 the kids were dancing to a different tune. Now their Dansette record players were pumping out the sound of American rock'n'roll from the likes of Bill Haley, Buddy Holly, Eddie Cochran and Elvis Presley. In this picture a girl gives a demonstration of rock'n'roll dancing at The Savoy Hotel.*

A barber's shop in Tottenham Court Road, London, applies the latest styles: 'Not so much of the short back and sides, thanks; give me one of those Elvis quiffs.' The age of the haircut being used as a weapon against your parents had dawned.

It's the early 1960s and men and women from the Caribbean dressed in their Sunday best pass through immigration at Victoria Station, London. They were wanted to work for London Transport and the Health Service among other enterprises, and one of the people who invited them into the country was Minister of Health Enoch Powell, later famous for his anti-immigration sentiments.

Bobby Charlton, one of the most famous footballers in Britain, plays with a group of young lads in the streets of his home town, Ashington, Northumberland. At the time Charlton was recovering from the Munich air crash of 1958, a tragedy that touched the hearts of the whole country.

Above *Sikh kids and their white friends pose for* Picture Post *in 1955. The British Nationality Act of 1948 gave subjects of the British Empire the right to live and work in the UK. Indian immigrants added greatly to life in the UK, not least by introducing a hot new taste to the nation as curry became the favourite meal out for millions.*

Right *Contestants packed in for an evening's bingo at the Trocadero Cinema in London's Elephant and Castle. Bingo replaced the dance hall as the place to go for your weekly fix of thrills and entertainment, but it was a far more compulsive pastime, and there were concerns about the nation's housewives blowing their housekeeping money.*

Still maintaining the traditions of the landed gentry, albeit via a more modern medium, the Hon. Lilah Charlotte Sarah White, heiress to the 16th-century Holdenby House in Northamptonshire, which once belonged to King James I, is arranged Gainsborough-style with her husband and children for a family portrait.

Toolmaker Ray Willis mows perfect stripes into the lawn of his semi-detached council house, while his wife and child chat to the neighbour over the fence. Council houses gave many people their own plot of land for the first time and the garden became a place to unwind, socialize and unleash one's creative talents.

A multi-tasking young mother brings her baby to work patrolling a busy road in east London. Lollipop men and women were introduced in 1953 to relieve the police force of the responsibility of helping pedestrians safely across the road, providing valuable part-time work for people with other obligations.

A garden plot development of the greener kind. Patricia Llewellyn of Newent in Gloucestershire trims the outstanding feature of her family home: a giant bush shaped into a house. The British obsession with gardening could lead to some eccentric creations, but people were also selling off garden land to cash in on the real estate value.

Certain traditions would have the British glued to their televisions and radio sets. This is one of them: the Third Round draw for the FA Cup in 1967, conducted here by Football Association executives David Wiseman and RH Brough. The FA Cup Final was one of the few sporting events to be broadcast live on TV.

East End gangster Ronnie Kray faces the realization that his criminal days are over. He and his twin brother Reggie were part of the fabric of Cockney life in the 1960s, either keeping order and maintaining values or ripping people off and spreading fear, depending on your standpoint.

By the 1970s the taste for flamboyance was being given full rein, both in public and in the home, as feathers, furs and leopard skin prints became all the rage. This is Gertrude Shilling, mother of hat designer David Shilling, with some of his outrageous creations.

Park Hill flats in Sheffield – built between 1957 and 1961, these were typical of the high-rise buildings of that period. In 1998, they were given Grade II listed status, making them (collectively) the largest listed building in Europe. The flats were referenced in the Pulp song 'Sheffield Sex City' and they were also the location for Harvey and Gadget's gaff in This Is England 90*. They are currently being re-modernized.*